ISBN (paperback): 979-8-88759-133-9
ISBN (ebook): 979-8-88759-134-6

"World's Greatest Mom
Ercilia Valburn"

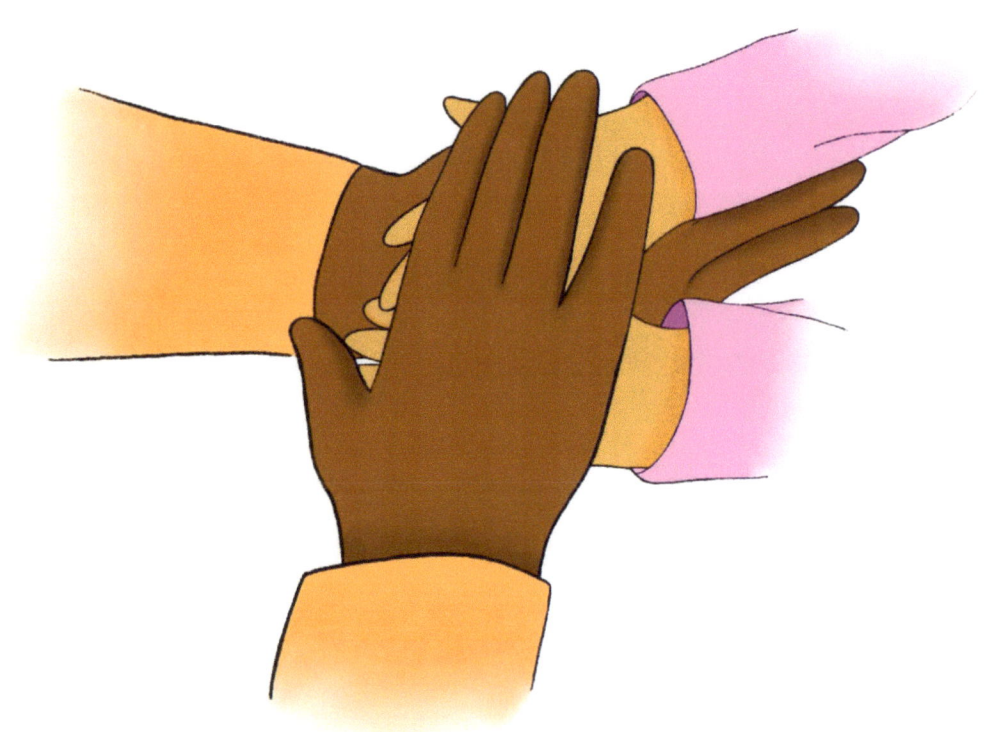

May 3, 1951 - April 25, 2020

Viola's
H~~u~~rt Heartfelt Words

Viola had no clue just how powerful her words were. Every day she had something negative to say. Things like:

"I CAN'T.."
"I DON'T KNOW HOW.."
"I'M TOO SMALL.."
"NO ONE CARES.."

Were some of the things she often said.

"WHAT AN IDIOT!" She uttered underneath her breath after Mr. Rogers called on Mark in class instead of her. And when he gave the wrong answer to the math problem, she huffed and puffed.

She yelled at her little sister during dinner time, when she accidently spilled juice all over the table while trying to pour a cup for herself.

That night before bed time, Momma came into Viola's room to talk to her about her attitude.

"STICKS AND STONES BREAK BONES. AND SO DO WORDS. THEY HURT, TOO", MOMMA SAID QUIETLY. "WORDS ARE NOT MEANT FOR MAKING SOMEONE FEEL SMALL. NOT FOR HURTING SOMEBODY'S FEELINGS. NOT EVEN FOR TRYING TO CONTROL SOMEBODY TO GET THEM TO DO WHAT YOU WANT," SHE SAID.

"BUT THEY ARE MEAN TO ME FIRST!"

MOMMA SMILED THAT KIND OF SMILE VIOLA LOVED.
"DO YOU KNOW WHY I NAMED YOU VIOLA? BECAUSE YOU'RE AS PRECIOUS TO ME AS A FLOWER. AND LIKE FLOWERS, YOU ARE MEANT TO BLOSSOM."

That night Viola thought hard about just how powerful her words were. And about how much her heart was in a bad place.

The next morning during breakfast, instead of watching her sister struggle to pour juice in her glass, Viola said to her, "WAIT, I CAN HOLD THE CUP WHILE YOU POUR. YOU CAN DO IT," SHE SAID WITH A SMILE.

At recess instead of saying mean things to Trish, she complimented her on how well she jumped rope.

And during class she waited patiently to be called and when her teacher didn't pick her to answer, she shrugged and said to herself, "maybe next time." Then she gave a thumbs-up to Billy when he answered correctly.

Viola understands now that Words can change your destiny in life.
Words can change not just your world but others' worlds.
People change people with their words.
So fill your heart and your words with love and kindness.

www.ingramcontent.com/pod-product-compliance
Lightning Source LLC
Chambersburg PA
CBHW040814120626
46547CB00004B/549